Improving Your Child's Self-Image

DR. BOB LAURENT

LIFEJOURNEY
BOOKS

Improving Your Child's Self-Image

LifeJourney Books is an imprint of David C. Cook
Publishing Co.
David C. Cook Publishing Co., Elgin, Illinois 60120
David C. Cook Publishing Co., Weston, Ontario
Nova Distribution, Ltd., Torquay, England

Edited by Brian Reck
Cover design by Bob Fuller
First printing, 1991
Printed in the United States of America
95 94 93 92 91 5 4 3 2 1

Library of Congress Cataloging in Publication Data

Laurent, Bob.
Improving Your Child's Self-Image/Bob Laurent.
    p. cm. — (Helping Families Grow series)
ISBN: 1-55513-661-3
1. Teenagers—Religious life. 2. Self-perception—
Religious aspects—Christianity. 3. Self-perception in
adolescence. 4. Parenting—Religious aspects—
Christianity.   I. Title.   II. Series: Helping Families
Grow.
BV4531.2.L3854   1991
248.8'45—dc20   91-26513
                                             CIP

More than once I have received a teen-written letter that I wished could have found its way into the hands—and hearts—of the parents before it reached mine.

Dear Bob,
I saw you this past weekend at the New York State Youth Convention. I really wanted to talk to you, but I chickened out. I find it easier to write things on paper.

I've been in a depression since school started. These past few weeks have gotten so bad that suicide has become dominant in my thoughts. It is really scaring me because I don't want to die, but I do at the same time. I cry myself to sleep just about every night, praying at the same time that God will let me die.

There are many things that have led to it. My father's work has become hard for him, so that when he comes home, he's always in a bad mood. He and my mother fight a lot. It gets to the point where she has started to cry, and I've never seen her cry before. The rest of us are really edgy because of that, so we fight too.

I'm doing bad in school, so I'm getting a lot of pressure from my teachers, and I can't handle it right now. My first report card came today, and I haven't shown my parents yet. I'm afraid to.

Another thing that has gotten to me is that I am eighteen years old and I have never had a real boyfriend. I guess it's because I'm so ugly! If I were a guy, I wouldn't want me, either.

Sometimes I feel like giving myself out sexually so I would feel like someone cared about me. I JUST WANT TO BE LOVED.

*Today was so bad for me, I just
wanted to go to sleep and never wake
up again, but that's too easy. If I
didn't know the consequences, I'd take
a knife to my wrist or a gun to my
head right now. Maybe someday I'll
get up the nerve to go through with it.
Maybe soon. Maybe tomorrow.
Everyday I get more nerve.*

*It's not like I haven't tried before—I
just haven't been lucky enough to die.*

*Thanks for letting me get my thoughts
out on paper. Please write me—I
NEED A FRIEND.*

In *Five Cries of Youth*, Merton Strommen
surveyed over 7,000 high school students
and discovered that the most commonly
voiced and intensely felt of the five cries was
the cry of self-hatred. Strommen reported
that the main contributing factors to this cry
were distress over personal faults, lack of
self-confidence, and low self-regard.[1]

In a survey I gave to teens, I tried to
measure this problem with the teens in my
study to see if there was a correlation
between a poor self-image and rejecting religion. I found low self-esteem to be the
fourth highest predictor of teen alienation

from the church. Typical responses from the 400 random students surveyed were:

> *"I am an attractive person." (disagree)*

> *"I do poorly in sports and games." (agree)*

> *"I am a morally weak person." (undecided)*

> *"I am satisfied to be just who I am." (strongly disagree)*

> *"I am not happy with myself." (agree)*

> *"I am not loved by my family." (undecided)*

THE LONELINESS FACTOR

Craig Ellison claims, "Among all the problems facing teenagers, loneliness is one of the most important." A professor of psychology at Simpson College, he conducted research among fifteen to nineteen year olds. In his estimation, there are two critical causes of loneliness among teenagers:

> 1. *Teens feel a lack of belonging or fitting in.*

> 2. *Teens feel that no one cares enough to understand them.*[2]

I agree with Ellison that teens are particularly susceptible to feeling isolated from God, parents, peers, and especially from themselves. A lack of belonging in any of these key relationships or the sense of being misunderstood can produce destructive loneliness.

Do you remember what it was like to feel alone and misunderstood at a time in your life when you weren't sure who you were or what you were worth? Dennis Varden, sixteen years old, knew that feeling. He wrote this piece of prose just before he took his own life.

> *He always wanted to have things*
> *   explained,*
> *But no one cared.*
> *The teacher came and spoke to him.*
> *She told him to wear a tie like all the*
> *   other little boys.*
> *He asked, "What does it really*
> *   matter?"*
> *After that they drew.*
> *He drew all yellow—*
> *It was the way he felt about the*
> *   morning*
> *And it was beautiful.*
> *But the teacher came and looked at*
> *   him.*
> *"What's this?" she said.*

> "Why don't you draw something like
>   Ken's drawing?
> Isn't his picture beautiful?"
> After that his mother bought him a tie.
> And he always drew airplanes and
>   rocket ships
> Like everyone else.
> And he threw his old picture away.
> But he wasn't alive anymore.
> He was square inside and brown.
> And his hands were still.
> And he was like everyone else.
> And the things inside him that needed
>   saying
> Didn't need it anymore.
> It had stopped pushing.
> It was crushed.
> Stiff.
> Like everything else.

NOBODY AND NO BODY

At the same time that teenagers are feeling
that nobody cares or understands, they are
also taking a critical look at their bodies
and, more often than not, are further
depressed by what they see.

Elizabeth Hurlock in her book
Developmental Psychology notes that very few
adolescents experience body-cathexis, or
satisfaction with their bodies. She adds,

"This failure to be satisfied with who you are physically is one of the causes of unfavorable self-concepts and lack of self-esteem during the adolescent years."[3]

According to Hurlock, there are three basic body types accompanied by predictable levels of self-esteem. More than likely you will see your teen in one of them:

1. The *mesomorph*—"well-built"; having more muscular than adipose tissue, this teen usually finds personal and social success more easily than the other two body types.

2. The *endomorph*—obese; having more adipose than muscular tissue, this youth often is ridiculed by his peers and pitied by adults.

3. The *ectomorph*—"skinny"; with small muscles and little adipose tissue, this teen is often socially maladjusted and exhibits an obsession with his physical appearance.[4]

I can empathize with teens on this subject because I had such a struggle with accepting my own physique. I was the self-conscious ectomorph. With religious zeal I would descend to my basement nightly for a rendezvous with my no-money-back Charles Atlas course: push-ups, sit-ups, jumping jacks, and four-count burpies.

After working up a good sweat with the calisthenics, I got down to serious business with the weight-training. With all the strength I could muster, I powered that weight-lifting bar up, up, up, and jerked it cleanly over my head in triumph. Then I set the bar down, put the weights back on it, and rolled it into the corner. I was going to be the biggest, strongest athlete in my school!

One day during lunch hour, I was unintentionally standing near a group of the popular guys in the hallway, feeling insecure as usual and desperately wanting to fit in. Emerging from the cafeteria came a girl on whom I had a secret crush.

To my surprise, she walked right up to me and said, "Hi, Bob."

In front of the guys, I self-consciously stammered, "Uhh-h-h, H-Hi, Doris."

I had no idea what else to say and was relieved when everybody started in talking again. I felt good about her seeing me with those "cool dudes" and wished that there was something I could do to impress her. Just then the bell rang and, as things started to break up, Doris moved toward me and casually placed her hand on my right arm to say good-bye.

Instinctively my arm went into a rigid

flex, and she exclaimed in front of everybody, "Wow! You've really got a muscle there."

I should have left well enough alone, but without thinking I crowed, "Yeah, I've been working out. C'mon, Doris. Hit me in the stomach as hard as you want. It won't even hurt me."

This was too good to miss. Late for class or not, the crowd seemed to swell as it gathered around us. It was then that I remembered something—Doris was one of the best athletes in our school. She was not only pretty; she was strong.

"Are you serious, Bob? I can hit you as hard as I want?"

"No problem," I replied, but the beads on my forehead betrayed the quiver in my liver.

She reared back, wound up, and buried her fist in my middle; then she pulled back, waiting for me to fold.

I looked at her as straight as I could with crossed eyes and repeated through clenched teeth, "no problem!"

It seems to be a phenomenon of adolescence that no matter how intelligent a teen is, he often feels very dumb; no matter how attractive, she often feels ugly; no matter how many people are concerned about them, they often feel unloved.

DEFINING THE HEALTHY SELF-IMAGE

Stanley Coopersmith suggests four components of a teenager's healthy self-image:

1. *Significance*—Your teens need to feel important to people who matter to them.

2. *Competence*—They must believe that they can do something well that makes a genuine contribution and is important to them.

3. *Power*—They need to feel that they have some control over their lives—that they have some decision-making capacities.

4. *Virtue*—They must believe that they are doing what they know to be right.[5]

Coopersmith has dealt with the social, physical, mental, and moral aspects of self-esteem, but he has neglected the spiritual. As a Christian educator, I would add a fifth component to his construct:

5. *Peace*—They must feel that their search for purpose and meaning in life has found its object in a personal experience with God in Jesus Christ.

Parents would scarcely be human if they didn't worry about the hard moral choices that their teens are facing every day in their absence. But ironically, the parents who are most worried about the ethical behavior of their teenagers are often the same ones who have, by engendering low self-esteem in their teens, made it very difficult for them to make good choices.

Stone and Church remind us that "it is not usually the person who has developed self-respect who turns into a doormat or a punching-bag for others."[6] It is unlikely that a teen with poor self-image will consistently have the strength of will to say no to drugs, premarital sex, drinking, and other negative options readily available to today's teenagers.

In his book, *Human Development in Western Culture*, Bernard states, "When children feel they are worthy of consideration, when limits are firm but established without parental condemnation, when encouragement rather than censure follows errors, the individual achieves a [strong] self-image. . . . It is this self-image that develops the internalization of moral codes and becomes one's conscience. . . . Basic to the establishment of a set of ethical values is a strong self-concept."[7]

WHAT PARENTS CAN DO

Even though your teen has to drive the old family station wagon and still shares a room with his little brother, if self-respect keeps his head held high, then you are a parent who should be content.

Even though you can't afford to buy her the latest styles with the right labels, and she may never be elected to the homecoming court, if she likes who she is and is excited about who she is becoming, then you are a parent who should be grateful.

If you do nothing else for your teens but equip them with confidence to, as James Cavanaugh writes, "live among the wolves," then you are a parent who should be revered.

"If you desire to be a helper of young people—a counselor in the best sense of the word, regardless of your technical training— here is one of your most vital tasks. You must help teenagers to accept themselves, to like themselves, to be glad they are who they are, to realize their value."[8]

How do you begin? Here are several things you can do to help build self-esteem in your teenagers:

1. Give them a sense of belonging.

"Once you were less than nothing; now you are God's own. Once you knew very little of God's kindness; now your very lives have been changed by it" (I Peter 2:10, LB).

Fitting into most of the social groups which make up the teenager's world almost always depends upon performance, looks, economic standing, or conformity. If your son is athletic enough, he is sure to find acceptance among the school "jocks." If your daughter is attractive, other-centered, and willing to conform to the American dating system, she can count on popularity among her peers.

There is only one group which does not—or at least should not—insist that teens measure up to its expectations before they are accepted: that is the family. It is possible for you to make your home that one place where your teenagers can fit in—in spite of an acne problem, empty wallet, fumbled football, bouts with depression, or an inability to grasp advanced algebra.

2. Resist the urge to recount your former successes.

"Speak only what is helpful for building others up according to their needs" (Ephesians 4:29b).

Zig Ziglar reminds us that when we rehearse our accomplishments from the past with our teens, "time dramatically improves [our] performance."[9] It is not uncommon for teens to become so discouraged with trying to live up to the quixotic stories and embellished achievements of their parents' past that they opt for destructive behavior.

Competing with the past, even if it is not an illusion, is too unrealistic a burden to lay on any teenager. So avoid the temptation to finish any sentence which begins with, "What do you mean you can't do it? Why, when I was your age—" or "I'm not one to brag, but—."

Your teens are bound to learn about your past laurels from old high school yearbooks, casual banter at family reunions, and diaries that turn up when you pack to move to a new house. If they discover your credits on their own, it is liable to endear you to them and give them a sense of healthy pride. But if you preach your past to them, do not be surprised by their resentment and alienation. Better that you discretely share your blunders than your boasts with your teenagers.

3. Caution them frequently that no one can steal their self-worth without their permission.

"It is God himself who has made us what we are and given us new lives from Christ Jesus" (Ephesians 2:10a, LB).

Neither you nor your teen is responsible for how others mistreat you, but you are accountable for how you react to slander, unjust criticism, and a vindictive spirit.

I had a student with a history of low self-esteem. He was aware of his susceptibility to depression triggered by anyone who criticized his efforts. We talked often about how his true self-worth was derived not from his performance, nor from the opinions of others, but from the fact that God had made him who he was. He had to stop allowing people or circumstances to steal his self-esteem.

One day in my office, I saw the lights go on in his head and a smile come across his face. It was not long afterwards that I heard he had placed a poster with three meaningful words over the bookshelf in his dorm room: Don't allow it!

Saint Augustine once observed, "People travel to wonder at the height of mountains, at the huge waves of the sea, at the long courses of the rivers, at the vast compass of the ocean, at the circular motion of the stars—and they pass by themselves without wondering."[10]

4. It's never too late to focus on your teenager's inner qualities.

"Be beautiful inside, in your hearts, with the lasting beauty of a gentle and quiet spirit which is so precious to God" (I Peter 3:4, LB).

We learned not to expect much in the way of physical attractiveness in our newborns for the first few weeks. Though they grow into fine looking children, each of our babies has been characterized by a head remarkably misshapen from its trip down the birth canal, a scalp as hairless as a billiard ball, and a funny little scowl that could curdle Similac. Cabbage Patch "preemies" have nothing on any of them.

So when our third child was born, I stood outside the hospital nursery window watching the nurse bathe her, thanking God for the smooth delivery, rejoicing in her good health, and praying for God to help us raise our daughter to be a committed Christian woman. Presently a fellow member of the church softball team came along to view the baby and congratulate me.

It was humorous for me to see him taking in that lopsided head, bald pate, wrinkled brow, and toothless scowl. Not knowing me very well, I'm sure he felt that he had to say something appropriate. He went beyond the call of duty.

"Hey, hey! What a beauty, huh? You're going to have a hard time keeping the guys away from that one. She's going to be a real heartbreaker!"

I knew that he meant no harm, but his comment got me thinking about the imbecilic system we have for evaluating human worth in this country. Almost from the day of their births, we condition our sons and daughters to believe that their self-worth is wrapped up in their physical appearance.

I overheard a young woman say that girls do not spend all that time and money on cosmetics because they are dumb or vain. On the contrary, they are intelligent enough to know that guys can see better than they can think!

One of the greatest lessons a child can learn is the meaning behind the verse, "The Lord does not see as man sees. Man looks at the outward appearance, but the Lord looks at the heart" (1 Samuel 16:7). It would be a good idea, when we are with our teens, if we could focus on things which last. Perhaps if we took every opportunity to compliment them on their character, integrity, and the fruit of the Spirit as it is evidenced in their lives (see Galatians 5:22, 23), we might see them better handle their struggle with self-esteem.

5. Help them experience satisfaction and find balance with their physical appearance.

"Honor God with your body" (I Corinthians 6:20).

As crucial as it is to encourage your teen to focus on his internal qualities, the fact is that there will probably be times when he can't see the "eternal" because the "temporary" is driving him to distraction (see II Corinthians 4:18: "So we fix our eyes not on what is seen, but on what is unseen. For what is seen is temporary, but what is unseen is eternal").

Having a teenager who is inordinately vain about his good looks is a problem. But is it less vain or destructive for a teen to be self-consumed with what he considers to be a physical flaw? I was extremely self-conscious and rendered socially dysfunctional in my early teen years by a chipped front tooth. After being teased by some kids at school about my "Bucky Beaver" grin, it became difficult for me to look people straight on when talking with them, and I eventually developed a crooked smile which remains with me today. My confidence level skyrocketed the weekend I had my teeth capped.

Whether you need to connect with an orthodontist for braces, an optometrist for contact lenses, a dermatologist for skin care, or even a plastic surgeon for help with a crooked nose, your teen's appreciation will make the expense worth it. It may free them up to go deeper when they are no longer plagued by a surface problem.

6. Remind them often of their inestimable worth.

"This is love: not that we loved God, but that he loved us and sent his Son as an atoning sacrifice for our sins" (I John 4:10).

I believe that it is God's desire that our teens value themselves in accordance with the price He has placed upon them. Your teenager is worth the death of Jesus Christ.

My sixteen-year-old son and I have a better understanding of that price because of a severely broken leg he suffered in a skiing accident when he was seven. For some reason there was no doctor available to set his bone on that raw February evening, so the decision was made to get him through the night with pain shots.

My nerves were on edge and my heart breaking with compassion as I sat in his darkened hospital room, listening to his quiet weeping turn to crying and eventually to feverish screaming. I felt totally helpless and gladly would have offered both of my legs for breaking if it would have alleviated the smallest part of his suffering.

Eventually, the pain was so intense and his fear of another hypodermic needle so vivid that he called me over to his bed. "Dad," he begged me, "you've got to promise me something!"

"What is it, son?" I replied, unable any longer to restrain my own tears.

"Don't let them stick me again!" he implored.

Scarcely a moment later, the nurse called me into the hallway and said, "Mr. Laurent, your son is waking this whole wing up. I have instructions to help him get to sleep."

I was relieved to hear that and wondered why they hadn't done so earlier. "Fine," I answered. "How are you going to do it?"

"I have to give him another injection. I need you to hold him down for me."

I pinned my son's spindly arms to the bed as the nurses whipped the sheet off his body and, for the fifth time that night, jabbed him in his bottom with the hypodermic.

His eyes were as big as saucers as he stared at me and let out a scream that pierced me like cold steel: "DA-A-A-A-A-ADD!"

For the first time in my life, I understood the Father's side of the Cross.

The day before His death at Golgotha, Jesus informed His best friends that he would be crucified and that, in the end, even they would betray him. They were vehement in their denial and pledged their loyalty to Him. In view of what happened on Friday, His next words surely came from the human side of the God-Man. "But I will not be alone, for my Father will be with me."

Jesus spoke several times as He hung on the Cross for six hours between Heaven and Hell. But to me, His most poignant speech occurred at the moment He fully realized the price which sin was to exact. Bleeding to death for the sins of the world, He became aware of something which had never happened since before the dawn of time. "My God! My God! Why have you forsaken me?"

Did God the Father hear his only Son crying, "DA-A-A-ADD!" when, because Jesus became my sin, His own father turned away from Him?

If I, having been created in the image of God, instinctively was ready to sacrifice all of my limbs that night just to repair my son's leg, what might the Father-heart of God felt on the dark afternoon His Son was murdered? The more basic question, though, is, why did He allow it?

The answer for you and your teenager is that you both are worth the death of Jesus Christ. You are that much loved.

TEARING DOWN THE WALLS

Many family counselors cite a simple lack of understanding between parents and teens as the major reason for the generation gap. Expecting parents to understand their teenagers may be as unrealistic as expecting your teen to put gas in the family car. No matter how hard you try or how many books you read on adolescent psychology, your own teens will, in many ways, remain a mystery to you.

You will never understand, for example, how your teen can break his school record in the hundred meter dash when his time from the breakfast table to the lawn mower could be measured with a sundial.

You will be mystified that your teen can spend two hours on the phone covering every imaginable subject and then come up mute during family devotions.

The riddle of the Sphinx is easier to decipher than observing teens who can get up at 5 A.M. to jog eight miles, lift weights for two hours every evening, never miss a chance to steal a base, make a lay-up, or catch a pass . . . yet need to be driven to the garbage can.

Still, whether we understand each other or not, the generation gap can be spanned. God has a good track record for removing barriers and reconciling His children to one another. There is no reason for the parent/teen years to be characterized by rebellion and mutual hostility. I am convinced that by the time you have weathered pierced ears and paper routes, driver's training and dating anxiety, Sunday morning battles for the bathroom and Sunday night term papers, you and your high school graduate can part as friends who want to see each other again as often as possible. Paul wrote to the Ephesians,

> "For he himself is our peace, who has made the two one and has destroyed the barrier, the dividing wall of hostility. . . . His purpose was to create in himself one new man out of the two, thus making peace, and in this one body to reconcile both of them to God through the cross, by which he put to death their hostility." (Ephesians 2:14, 15)

As a fellow parent of teenagers, I encourage you to "follow God's example in everything you do, just as a much-loved child imitates his father" (Ephesians 5:1, LB). I believe a final look at His example would serve as a good summary.

PARENTING A TEEN IS NOT YOUR JOB

On my son's fifth birthday, he received an inordinate amount of presents and attention from his friends, neighbors, and relatives. He was the focal point of a large party and he was enjoying every moment of it. Showing off for about a dozen of his playmates, he fell off his new bike and skinned his knees on the driveway. Picking him up quickly, I shut off his tears by reminding him of all the gifts that awaited him inside the house. That evening when I was tucking him in bed following our nightly wrestling match/pillow fight, it occurred to me that he had been doted on so much this birthday that his head might benefit from a little deflating. Acting on an impulse I asked,

"Son, you think your friends really love you, don't you?"

"Well, sure, Dad!" came his confident reply.

"And you think your Grandma and Grandpa love you, too, don't you?"

"Sure, Dad! Did you see that bike they gave me?"

"And son, you think that I really love you, don't you?"

"Sure, Dad!" came the expected answer.

"Well, son," I said with the tongue firmly planted in my cheek. "I don't love you. I don't love you at all."

As soon as those words escaped my lips, I wished that I had not said them. At first, his little face screwed up in confusion, and I thought he might cry. To my relief though, his frown was replaced by a smile, and he blurted out,

"Oh, yes, you do!"

"You're right! But how do you know that I love you?" I queried.

He thought for a moment and answered, "Because you got me a present too!"

"OK, but how else do you know that I love you?"

Searching his mind, he replied, "Because you wrestle with me, Dad!"

"That's great, son, but isn't there any other reason for you to know that I love you?"

The silence in the darkness of his bedroom was soon broken with a cry of, "That's easy, Dad! Today when I fell down, you were there to pick me up!"

When I shared this story with my wife, two key truths occurred to us. First, when we do something right in raising our children, we are most likely imitating the example that God the Father has given us. And secondly, in the best ways that we parents show love to our children, so our Heavenly Father cares for us. These truths should be particularly encouraging to the parents of teenagers.

The reason we are even able to follow His example in relating to our teens is not because of our own abilities as parents, but because He is at work within us. "For it is God who works in you to will and to act according to his good purpose" (Philippians 2:13).

Only three persons have ever been able to live the Christian life, let alone successfully raise Christian teenagers: God the Father, Christ the Son, and the Holy Spirit—and they dwell within you for that purpose (Colossians 2:9, 10). Your ultimate responsibility is to receive the forgiveness afforded you by the death of our Lord Jesus via personal repentance, begin parenting in the power of the Holy Spirit, and leave the results up to God. For you, a Christian parent, to live is Christ, not Christ-like (Philippians 1:21).

It is as self-defeating as it is unscriptural for you to whip yourself into a frenzy of guilt over your failures as a parent. The only unscarred experts on teenagers never had any. The only parent who made no mistakes raising his teen was God—and He loves you: "Cast all your anxiety on Him, for He cares for you" (I Peter 5:7).

WHAT IF GOD TOLD YOU HE DIDN'T LOVE YOU?

What if tonight in a bad dream you saw God sitting on His throne reading a scroll entitled, "Parents Who Have Blown It with Their Teen?" His eyes scan the lists, past the Hefners, the Hitlers, and the Huxleys, until they come to rest on your name. God looks up and says to you, "I don't love you. I don't love you at all."

Such a scene would not only be a nightmare, it would be a lie. "Oh, yes, you do!" you would cry. "I know that you love me—for three reasons!"

1. *"Because You gave me a present, God. No one ever loved me enough to give me what You have."*

The magnitude of His gift to us parents became more vivid to me a few years ago at the funeral of the wife of one of my best friends. At age thirty-one, with a five-year-old and a two-year-old down the hall and her baby of four weeks in the room next door, Karen accidentally electrocuted herself with her hairdryer in the bathroom. Three days later at the memorial service I listened as her pastor read notes that she had written in the margins of her Bible.

After a few moments, he felt compelled to stop reading and joined his congregation in a poignant time of weeping.

Through my own tears, I glanced around the church and realized that everyone was crying. I had never experienced corporate grief like that before. "Why," I wondered, "is this funeral so much harder than any other I've ever attended?"

The answer came to me later that day after Karen's husband movingly observed, "She lived long enough for so many people to get to know her and love her, and yet she had so many years ahead of her to live. She was cut down in the middle of her life."

"Cut down in the middle of life"—that phrase surfaced again in the car trip home from the funeral when I realized that it also described the death of Jesus Christ. He lived long enough to endear Himself to thousands, yet had a lifetime of memories ahead. When He was agonizing in the Garden the night before His death and asking, "Father, if you are willing, take this cup from me" (Luke 22:42), might He not have been thinking, "There is so much left to do. There are so many lepers still to be touched, Pharisees who remain uncon-vinced, tax collectors to be saved, families to be restored, and children to be embraced. There is so much more life to be lived."

It was because He loved you and me that He finished His prayer with, ". . . yet not my will, but yours be done," and went out to be cut down in the middle of His life—for the sins of the parents and teenagers of that day as well.

It is because you are much-loved by God and worth the death of Jesus Christ that you can love your teenagers through their rebellion without feeling that you must win the parent/teen conflicts. Most Christian parents are aware of John 3:16 ("For God so loved the world that He gave. . . ."), but few are aware of I John 3:16: "This is how we know what love is: Jesus Christ laid down his life for us. And so we ought to lay down our lives for our brothers."

What would Karen have given to have the chance to see her babies grow to maturity—to know her children as teenagers and friends? Cut down in the middle of life. There is a harder fate than raising teens.

"Yes, You could tell me that You don't love me, but I know that You do because,

2. *You wrestle with me, God. You didn't gift me with parenting and then leave me to my own*

devices. You are in my world and actively care about the most mundane of my parental responsibilities. I can make it because I know You will live up to Your name, Immanuel, 'God with us.' "

Shortly after the premature death of our third child, my wife and I were commiserating with each other while reading the beloved Shepherd's Psalm. Fighting deep despair, we were looking for help from Scripture in dealing with the pain of separation. Joyce noticed a significant word in a well-known passage. "Yea, though I walk through the valley of the shadow of death," she read. "Robert, I believe this is God's word to us. We are going to get through this together."

Then I recognized the reason we were going to make it through this ordeal together: ". . . for Thou art with me." The central glory of the gospel and the good news for us as the parents of teenagers is that "The tabernacle of God is among men" (Revelation 21:3). When John wrote, "The Word became flesh and dwelt among us," he used a remarkable word which can be translated, "pitched His tent" among us. God has moved in for the duration. You are not parenting alone, even if you are a single parent. His promise is still true: "Never will I leave you; never will I forsake you" (Hebrews 13:5b).

"You could tell me that You don't love me, Lord, but I know that You do because,

3. *When I fell down, You were there to pick me up.*"

The reason a parent can "fall seven times, and rise again" (Proverbs 24:16) is because He will be there to lift you up if you call upon Him for help. But there is little He can do when we will not admit that we have fallen. Of the miserable state of his people in Egypt, God told Moses, "I have heard them crying out . . . so I have come down to rescue them" (Exodus 3:7, 8).

It makes little sense to me that we wait so long to confess our humanity and need for help when He stands ready to marshal all the forces of Heaven to come to our aid. Pride is a hard taskmaster and robs us of resources that a parent of teenagers must have. Sometimes it is as if we are stubbornly holding on to our pathetic, little brown paper bag containing a limp, bologna sandwich when God is offering us a marvelous banquet feast. Likewise, our inability to swallow our pride before our teens and make the first move toward reconciliation with them might be keeping us from a "family-agape feast."

Elizabeth Elliot once wrote to her daughter,

> *Who is it you marry? You marry a sinner. There's nobody else to marry. . . . Acceptance of him—all of him—includes acceptance of his being a sinner. He is a fallen creature in need of the same kind of redemption all the rest of us are in need of. What a lot of heartbreak would be avoided if we could concentrate on the essentials and skip the rest. How much more we could relax with one another and enjoy all there is to enjoy."* [11]

Parents and teens would do well to remember this advice when tempted to hold grudges or harbor bad feelings for one another. Two fundamentals for emancipating our teenagers are judiciously giving them room to fail and experience the consequences of their decisions, and honestly admitting our own faults in their presence.

It is a liberating feeling to know that someone important to you still loves you (in fact, may love you even more) in spite of their awareness of your weaknesses. Driving to a friend's home during summer vacation, I was reminded by my wife of the major reason I love to be with my family. After getting us hopelessly lost in the northern woods of Michigan, I finally relented and pulled into a gas station for new directions. I followed the station attendant's advice for a few miles, but then my stubbornness flared up and I announced that we were going to try a different "shortcut" that I was sure would work. The moaning of Joyce and my teens only deepened my resolve to redeem myself.

It wasn't long before I was looking for moss on the trees and peering for familiar constellations. It was humiliating to have to pull into another station and get a different set of directions. This time, I drove in silence, and my family was wise enough not to break it.

After sorting out my emotions and reflecting on my juvenile behavior, I finally admitted, "You know what really bothers me about this whole thing? It's not just that I got us lost, or even that I'm responsible for wasting so much of our vacation time. You guys know what it is, don't you?"

Their reply was more silence, but I had to finish. "It's that you, my own family, saw me act like an absolute jerk back there!"

That was it. I would say no more and they knew it. My wife waited an appropriate amount of time, then reached over to pat me on the shoulder and spoke for the whole family: "That's okay, honey. We already knew you were like that."

There is no freedom like being loved by someone who really knows you.

"O Lord, you have searched me and you know me (Psalm 139:1).

You are familiar with all my ways (Psalm 139:3).

Your love, O Lord, endures forever" (Psalm 138:8).

We have come quite a distance together in this booklet. For two reasons I have great hope for you as the parent of a teenager: because you care, and because you can do all things through Christ who strengthens you.

I leave you with a final thought which summarizes much of what has gone before. I have asked many youth pastors in the past decade, "What is the biggest problem you face in ministering to teens?" Time and again I have heard them reply, "Parents with little faith in Christ and little time for their teens."

This situation does not have to be.

Christian parents can be their teenagers' greatest asset. But teens will continue to leave the church if parents and the church do not pull together and work at eliminating barriers to the faith of their teens. And that takes time. I have a friend who wrote the following words to a famous old hymn of the church.

> *I ran today where Jesus walked, in*
> *days of long ago.*
> *Raced down each little path He knew*
> *I've a schedule, as you know.*
> *I'm always busy,*
> *I keep the pace*
> *I hurry everywhere.*
> *I ran today where Jesus walked.*
> *And missed His presence there.*

ENDNOTES

1. Merton Strommen, *Five Cries of Youth*, New York: Harper and Row, 1974.
2. Craig Ellison, "Lonely Teens." *Christian Herald*, May 1979, pp. 15-18.
3. Elizabeth Hurlock, *Developmental Psychology: A Life-Span Approach*, 5th edition, New York: McGraw-Hill Book Company, 1980, p. 228.
4. Ibid. pp. 117, 187.
5. Stanley Coopersmith, *The Antecedents of Self-Esteem*, San Francisco, Calif.: W.H. Freeman, 1967, p. 163.
6. L. Joseph Stone and Joseph Church, *Childhood and Adolescence*, New York, Random House, 1957, p. 126.
7. William Bernard, *Human Development in Western Culture*, p.399.
8. Roger Dudley, *Why Teenagers Reject Religion*, Washington, D.C., Review and Herald Publishing Association, 1978, p.112.
9. Zig Ziglar, *Raising Positive Kids in a Negative World*, Oliver Nelson Publishing, Nashville, Tenn.: 1985, p. 158.
10. Ibid p. 158.
11. Elisabeth Elliot, *Growing Together*, September 1982, p. 6.

HELPING FAMILIES GROW SERIES

- *Communicating Spiritual Values Through Christian Music*
- *Equipping Your Child for Spiritual Warfare*
- *Family Vacations that Work*
- *Helping Your Child Stand Up to Peer Pressure*
- *How to Discover Your Child's Unique Gifts*
- *How to Work With Your Child's Teachers*
- *Helping Your Child Love to Read*
- *Improving Your Child's Self-Image*
- *Preparing for Your New Baby*
- *Should My Child Listen to Rock Music?*
- *Spiritual Growth Begins At Home*
- *Surviving the Terrible Teenage Years*

ABOUT THE AUTHOR

For more than 20 years, Dr. Bob Laurent has ministered to teens. He holds a Ph.D. in Religious Education, specializing in adolescent psychology. Dr. Laurent is the author of *Keeping Your Teen in Touch with God* and the recently released *Bringing Your Teen Back to God*. He currently teaches Bible at Judson College in Elgin, Illinois, where he lives with his wife, Joyce Ann, and their four children.